Y0-BQX-144

LEVEL A, PART 1

A Pig Can Jig

by Donald Rasmussen and Lynn Goldberg

Columbus, Ohio

A Division of The McGraw·Hill Companies

SRA/McGraw-Hill

A Division of The **McGraw·Hill** *Companies*

Send all inquiries to:
SRA/McGraw-Hill
250 Old Wilson Bridge Road
Suite 310
Worthington, Ohio 43085

Printed in the United States of America.

ISBN 0-02-683997-0

1 2 3 4 5 6 7 8 9 0 RRC 05 04 03 02 01 00 99

Contents, Part 1

man

Dan

ran

fan

can

I
■
the

I ran.

Dan ran.

The man ran.

I can fan.

Dan can fan.

The man can fan.

The man can fan.

I can fan the man.

The man can fan Dan.

I can fan Dan.

Can Dan fan?

Can the man fan?

Can I fan?

Dan can fan.

The man can fan.

I can fan.

Can I fan the man?

I can fan the man.

Can the man fan Dan?

The man can fan Dan.

Can Dan fan the man?

Dan can fan the man.

Nan

pan

tan

van

to

7

Nan ran.

Nan ran to the van.

Nan ran to the tan van.

I ran.

I ran to the van.

I ran to the tan van.

9

I ran.

I ran to the pan.

Nan ran.

Nan ran to the pan.

Nan ran to the tan pan.

Nan can fan.

Can Nan fan the pan?

Can Nan fan the van?

Can Nan fan the man?

Nan CAN fan the man.

The Fan

Dan ran.

Nan ran.

Dan ran to the man.

Nan ran to the man.

The man can fan.

The man can fan Dan.

The man can fan Nan.

3

bad

dad   Dad

had

mad

pad

sad

a

13

I Can Fan

I had a fan.

I ran.

I ran to Dad.

I ran to fan Dad.

I ran to Nan.

I ran to fan Nan.

I can fan.

The Sad Man

The sad man ran.

The sad man ran to Nan.

Nan had a fan.

Nan can fan the sad man.

I Can Fan a Man

I can fan a sad man.

I can fan a tan man.

I can fan a bad man.

Can I fan a mad man?

The Bad Fan

Dad had a fan.

Dan ran to the fan.

Nan ran to the fan.

Can Dad fan Dan?

Can Dad fan Nan?

Dad had a bad fan.

Sad Dan!

Sad Nan!

MAD Dad!

The Pad

Nan had a pad.

Nan had a tan pad.

Dan ran.

Dan ran to the pad.

Dan had the tan pad.

Bad Dan!

Mad Nan!

bag

rag

tag

wag **Wag**

4

ragbag

and

Wag and I

I ran.

I ran to tag Wag.

Wag ran and ran.

Wag ran to a van.

I ran to the van.

I can tag Wag.

Wag

Wag ran to Dan.

Wag can tag Dan.

Wag ran to Nan.

Can Wag tag Nan?

Nan ran.

Wag ran to tag Nan.

Wag can tag Nan.

The Ragbag

Nan had a rag.

Nan had a ragbag.

Nan had a rag and a ragbag.

Wag ran to Nan and the ragbag.

Bad Wag had the ragbag.

Sad Nan had a rag.

Wag and the Bag

Dad had a bag.

Wag ran to Dad.

Wag had the bag.

Wag had the bag and ran.

Dad ran.

Dad ran to Wag.

Dad had a sad bag.

Tag

Nan! Nan!

Nan can

tag Dan!

Dan! Dan!

Dan can

tag Wag!

Wag! Wag!

Wag can

tag a man!

bat

cat

fat

hat

mat

pat   Pat

rat

sat

at

5

The Cat and the Rat

Dan and Nan had a fat cat.

Dan and Nan ran to a mat.

The fat cat ran to the mat.

The fat cat sat.

Dan and Nan sat to pat the cat.

A rat ran.

The fat cat ran at the rat.

The rat ran and ran.

Dan and Nan had the cat.

Dan and Nan sat to pat the cat.

The rat ran and ran and ran.

Pat at Bat

Dan had a bat.

Pat ran to Dan.

Pat had the bat.

Pat can bat.

Pat ran.

Dan had to tag Pat.

Dan ran to tag Pat.

Dan can tag Pat.

Dan had the bat.

Pat ran to tag Dan.

Pat can tag Dan.

Pat and Dan sat.

A Rat Ran

A rat ran to a mat

and sat!

A man ran to a bat

and sat!

A cat ran to a hat

and sat!

A rat and a man

and a cat, cat, cat

ran to a mat,

ran to a bat,

ran to a hat,

and sat, sat, sat!

cap

lap

map

nap

rap

tap

35

Tan, the Cat

Tan, the cat, sat.

Tan, the cat, had a nap.

Wag ran to Tan.

Wag ran to Tan and sat.

Wag had a nap.

Can Wag and Tan nap?

The Nap

Nan ran to a mat.

Nan had a nap.

Dan ran to Nan.

Dan had a bat.

Tap! Tap! Tap!

Dan can tap the bat.

Nan sat.

Nan ran at Dan.

Dan ran.

The Cap

Dan had a cap.

Dan had a tan cap.

Dan sat.

Dan had a nap.

Tap! Tap! Tap!

A fat cat ran.

A fat cat ran to the cap.

The fat cat had the cap.

Bad cat!

Sad Dan!

I Had a Bat

A-rat-a-tat-tat!

I had a bat.

A-rap-a-tap-tap!

A bat can rap.

A-rat-a-tat-tat!

I had a cat.

A-rap-a-tap-tap!

A cat can nap.

A-rat-a-tat-tat!

The bat sat to rap.

A-rap-a-tap-tap!

CAN the cat nap?

Maps, Caps, and Laps

I had a map.

Pat had a map.

Pat and I had maps.

I had a cap.

Pat had a cap.

Pat and I had caps.

I sat.

I had a LAP!

Pat sat.

Pat had a LAP!

Pat and I had maps,

and caps,

and laps!

44

ham

jam

Pam

Sam

am

of

7

I Am Tan

I am Tan.

I am a tan cat.

I ran to Pam.

Pam had a pan.

Pam had a pan of ham.

I had the ham.

I am a fat tan cat.

I Had a Can of Jam

I had a can of jam.

A can of jam I had.

I had a pan of ham.

A pan of ham I had.

I had the ham and jam.

The ham and jam I had.

I sat and had the ham

and the jam, jam, jam!

A Cat and a Bag

Sam and Pam had a mat.

Sam and Pam sat.

Pam had a tan bag.

A fat cat ran to the bag.

Tap! Tap! Tap!

The cat had the bag.

Sam ran to the cat.

The fat cat ran.

Sam had the bag.

Ham and Jam

Sam had a pan of ham.

Sam had a can of jam.

Sam had ham and jam.

A cat ran to Sam.

The cat had the ham.

Sad Sam had jam.

A Fat Cat

I am a fat cat.

A fat cat I am.

I ran and ran

to a pan of jam!

I am a fat cat.

A fat cat I am.

I sat and had

the pan of jam!

8

Hal	cab
pal	jab
Sal	
Al	

has

as

53

Al

I am Al.

I am Pam's pal.

I had a ham

as I ran to Pam.

I am Al.

I am Sam's pal.

I had jam

as I ran to Sam.

I am a pal.

A pal I am—

a pal of Pam's

and a pal of Sam's.

Wag at Hal's Cab

Hal has a cab.

Hal sat and sat.

Hal had a nap.

Wag ran to the cab.

Wag had to tap the cab.

Tap! Tap! Tap!

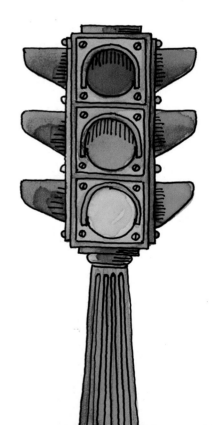

Wag had to jab Hal.

Jab! Jab! Jab!

Wag sat in Hal's lap.

Hal had to pat Wag.

Wag had a pal.

Hal and Wag ran the cab!

A Pal

I am a pal.

A pal I am.

I ran and ran.

I ran to Pam.

Pam has a pal.

Pam's pal I am.

I had to nap,

and ran to Pam.

59

Pattern Page

1 (page 1)	2 (page 7)	3 (page 13)
man	Nan	bad
Dan	pan	dad Dad
ran	tan	had
fan	van	mad
can		pad
	to	sad
I ■ the		a

Pattern Page

4 (page 21)	5 (page 27)	6 (page 35)
bag	bat	cap
rag	cat	lap
tag	fat	map
wag Wag	hat	nap
	mat	rap
ragbag	pat Pat	tap
and	rat	
	sat	
	at	

Pattern Page

7	8	9
(page 45)	(page 53)	(page 1)

7	8		9
ham	Hal	cab	bit
jam	pal	jab	fit
Pam	Sal		hit
Sam	Al		kit Kit
am			pit
of	has as		sit
			it
			Kitcat

Pattern Page

10 (page 9)	**11** (page 21)	**12** (page 29)
pin	big	did
tin	dig	hid
win	fig	lid
in	jig	rid
	pig	Sid
	wig	

his
is
■
into

began

was

Pattern Page

	13 (page 39)	14 (page 49)
him	if	dip
Jim		hip
Kim		lip
rim		rip
Tim		sip
		tip
		zip

said